THE
BUSINESS CASUAL
SURVIVAL GUIDE

30 LOOKS FOR MEN

EMMI SOROKIN

The Business Casual Survival Guide: 30 Looks for Men
Emmi Sorokin

Printed by CreateSpace
First Printing, 2013

ISBN-13: 978-0615925134
ISBN-10: 0615925138

Emmi Sorokin
www.emmisorokin.com

CONTENTS

May this book serve as a force
multiplier for your awesomeness.

–Emmi

MEET BRYAN

As I'm pacing the store's marble aisle in anticipation of Bryan, the gentleman who will be attending this wardrobe session begrudgingly and on his father's dime, the sharp squeak of his New Balance sneakers jolts me around, and my eyes behold him in all his Before-Emmi glory. I don't know where to pretend to not look first. Bryan's father had described him to me as a highly-intelligent 30-year-old, but one who also still wears what he did in college, hasn't cut his hair in years, and refuses to trim his shaggy beard. With Bryan actually walking toward me now, I realize that I'm going to have to utilize all of my Jedi mind tricks to succeed on my mission.

This mission—to find Bryan a small wardrobe of comfortable basics that he loves to wear and that make him feel like a rock star for his kind of business casual lifestyle—is fraught with challenges. First, it appears that Bryan doesn't actually see and appreciate what body he is dressing every morning. His jeans are at once too wide and too short for him, which provides everyone with a view of the white athletic socks clinging to his ankles. Above the waist, he is "complementing" his tech conference T-shirt with an oversized flannel shirt that is unbuttoned and hanging like a plaid robe.

Second, there is Bryan's mentality about how he dresses for the office: "I'm a software engineer, so what I wear to work really doesn't matter. The powers that be are happy when we show up in pants instead of shorts, so I usually opt for jeans and a T-shirt." Bryan had admitted this to me when we spoke on the phone at the urging of his father, and I have already developed a sense that Bryan doesn't trust me. In his eyes, I'm one of those people with the word "fashion" in her job title who wants to make him wear fancy clothes that he won't like. Proving him wrong is going to be fun.

Third, we have the hair and the beard. His scraggly ponytail wouldn't look good on anyone, and his massive amount of facial hair is the antithesis of a well-groomed, masculine and rugged beard. This one makes you take a step back out of fear that you're going to get caught in the crossfire of a crumb projectile shaking free from it. To top it all off, when I smile and reach out to shake Bryan's hand, he opens with, "We're not touching the beard."

I take a deep breath, focus on my vision of a well-coiffed and confident Bryan taking the stage at TED, and invite my newest client to take a look behind Door #1. As Bryan walks hesitantly into the fitting room, I see the familiar response—his fight-or-flight body posture relaxes, his furrowed brow gives way to a piqued curiosity, and he nods slightly as he reaches out and touches the super-soft, brushed cotton hoodie. "Hmmp, this isn't bad," he says quietly. This is the first sign of hope.

Over the next couple of hours, I watch Bryan slowly come out of his shell. He observes himself in the mirror in all the different clothes I had curated with his needs and preferences in mind, and as he sees himself in clothes that actually flatter his physique while at the same time feeling completely comfortable, his posture straightens and his body language becomes more self-assured. When he starts sneaking in some extra glances at his reflection near the end of our session, I can't help but notice his growing smile. (Or at least I thought it was a smile; the beard made it hard to see.)

By the time we leave the store, relations have improved remarkably, and there are 10 days of solid work looks in the bag. Bryan has tossed out what he came in wearing and is strutting outside in a casual, tailored button-down and new soft denim. I decide to seize the new but still tender bond of Bryan's trust and shove him into a cab for part two of the everybody-knew-this-was-coming-except-for-maybe-Bryan plan. We are off to State Street Barbers.

When we arrive at the high-end, old school-inspired barber shop, the manager, who knew I'd be coming in with a potential "runner," immediately places a Sam Adams in Bryan's hands. This allows us to get to the second trick we have up our sleeves—the hairstylist. She is hot and apparently allergic to any shirt that covers her belly button. Even if Bryan wants to leave the chair, I am hoping he can't leave the view.

Three beers later, the "simple trim" Bryan agreed to has turned into a full-scale haircut, and the BIG moment is now upon us. As if in a mirror standoff, Bryan sits in his chair staring steely-eyed at me and the hairstylist, and we stare back at his beard. "Well, what would you like to do?" my co-conspirator asks. With the assured command of the Godfather, I lift my finger to his chin and say, "Take it all off."

By the end of Bryan's straight-razor shave, the mid-riffed hair stylist, whose body language upon introduction to him had clearly said, "You want me to do what with this serial killer's hair?" is asking him if he is single, leaning in close, and completely flirting with him. Jaws are also agape throughout the barber shop, because underneath what was Bryan's hairy rebellion are some gorgeous facial features. Another case in the "hidden hot" files closed!

One month later Bryan texts me: he got a 12% salary bump, while his buddies in the cube averaged only 4% during the same review process. He was also commended for taking ownership of his professional image at work, and his bosses wanted him to know they really appreciated his effort and initiative in setting a new standard for his peers.

Like most men, Bryan didn't know what he was missing out on. Things seemed okay, and he was comfortable. Why go through the effort of making any changes? Because how you choose to step out of the house has a MASSIVE impact on the quality of your life. Don't take my word for it, though. Let's ask someone with a few more bestsellers under his belt than me, like Malcolm Gladwell.

THE IMPACT OF PERSONAL PRESENTATION ON QUALITY OF LIFE

Malcolm Gladwell and the Case of the Dubious Hairstyle

Chances are you've heard of Malcolm Gladwell—bestselling author, thought leader, and dubious hairstyle survivor. But not as well known is why he wrote his book *Blink*, an incredible read on the power of first impressions.

When Gladwell first reached the success of having a bestseller with *The Tipping Point*, he decided that he could relax a little, and he made one choice that, according to him, significantly altered his life in some alarming ways. What was that, you ask? Kill his neighbor? Beat a puppy and post it on YouTube? Nope, he grew his hair out all wild and curly. I'd show you the before and after pics, but in this crazy world we live in there are copyright laws, so you can either google it or trust me. With the new hairstyle, Gladwell started getting speeding tickets, which had never happened before in all his years of driving in New York City. He was even apprehended on the sidewalk under the erroneous suspicion of being a rapist. When Gladwell noticed that the police sketch depicted a criminal who happened to have curly hair but was also much younger, taller, and heavier than him, his eyes were opened to the power that first impressions can have on the quality of our lives, and he set out to write *Blink*.

The book explores how first impressions are made (what science calls rapid cognition), and how within moments of first viewing someone, we have made some pretty complex decisions about his or her social status, trustworthiness, and likeability. This process is evolutionary and involuntarily automatic. In the days of the early Homo sapiens, you needed to be able to tell right away whether the thing coming towards you out of the corner of your eye was a friend or a foe. If it took your ancestors five minutes to make these decisions, you wouldn't be here to tell about it. Today, with more information bombarding us every day, we rely on first impressions more heavily than ever, and the ones you leave can have profound effects on your life. They impact how much salary you can get away with asking for, how willing people are to follow along with what you say, and everything in between.

Psychological research abounds regarding the enormous role that clothing and grooming have in forming these first impressions. Here's where it gets really juicy, though. It's not just that clothing impacts how others view us; it impacts how we view ourselves.

In 2012, two researchers from Northwestern University, Hajo Adam and Adam Galinsky, published their research to support this notion. Specifically, after testing the attention to detail of subjects who were wearing what they thought was a doctor's lab coat versus those who thought they were wearing a painter's jacket, the performance of the former group was superior even though they were wearing the same white jacket. In other words, the simple act of wearing clothing that makes you feel confident can change your life, because your clothing influences how you feel about yourself and the work you do. The act of putting on the team jersey, race suit, or surgeon scrubs gets your game mode on and primes your mental pump for success.

Traditionally, the power suit has done that in business, but now that the majority of the workforce doesn't wear a suit every day, what are men to do? Is there a "power hoodie"?

WHY BUSINESS CASUAL IS SO HARD

Back in the days of *Mad Men*, life in the office was easy. In addition to drinking during the day and banging your secretary, you didn't need to deal with "business casual." Putting on a suit was paint-by-numbers. From a finite number of choices, you could plug in a suit jacket and slack and dress shirt and tie, and your mission was accomplished. If you were the type of gent who liked to dress it up, you added your favorite color pocket square and snazzy cufflinks. Not only was the system simple, but the structure of the jacket evened the playing field of flattering the man's physique. It emphasized the shoulders to help create the highly sought-after V shape (more on this later).

For the majority of the male workforce, the built-in safety net of the plug-and-play suiting model is now gone. In its place is a loosely defined and seemingly all-encompassing "business casual," and what men should wear varies dramatically by:

Industry: "Business casual" at a bank looks very different than it does at a tech startup. The blue blazers and khaki chinos are perfectly appropriate for the financial industry but look chumpy at a software startup, where a shirt with a collar would be considered dressing up.

Position: Within the same company, employees with different titles can have very different considerations they need to take into account. COOs interface with other C-level executives, board members, and investors, so they need to look sharp, but they can't be so dressed up that their attire forms a barrier with the field crew. IT managers also need to look polished but have clothes that can take a beating when they jump into a cable pit. Engineers can often dress more casually and comfortably in jeans and a T-shirt, but they can't look so disheveled that a visiting client's eyes would need to be shielded.

Zip code: What's considered appropriate in DC looks stiff in LA; what looks sharp in Miami seems loud and out of place in Boston. Showing individuality is great, but equally important is showing that you get and respect the culture in which you are doing business. Men who travel a lot for business typically need more than one set of location-appropriate clothing.

Add to these factors a perfect storm of more clothing brand options than ever before, disinterested or uneducated retail staff, and vague company dress code guidelines that define business casual as anything from a suit to jeans and a polo, and you can see why men cling to the perceived safety of the typical business casual uniforms even if they don't feel inspired by them. While this is understandable, it must be fixed. Why?

When you settle in your everyday clothes, you settle in life. You have to work at people thinking you're awesome, rather than having them know it from a glance. Not only are you making yourself an indistinguishable sheep, but you're also denying yourself the quality of life that comes with the confidence of swagger.

MEET ED

The path to swagger is different for each man I work with, but certain obstacles pop up time and time again and reveal valuable lessons when examined in context. With that in mind, hang on to the velvety sleeve of the Ghost of Style Past as we journey to the first year of my men's fashion career and meet Ed.

It's 7:30 a.m., which, if you're not winding down to go to bed, is way too early to be awake. But I am up, I am showered, and I am dressed, goddammit, all because I said I would be at this BNI networking breakfast. I'm clutching my coffee for dear life and chugging it in large messy gulps, and fortunately for me, everyone else seems to be too busy arranging the unnecessarily large piles of business cards that they brought along to notice my vampiric inhaling at the refreshment table. As the coffee hits my bloodstream, I correct my posture, wipe the dribble from my chin like a lady, and decide I'm ready to mingle! Did the universe feel my internal declaration?

"Hello!" I hear from behind me, in a chipper, I've-already-had-my-coffee-on-the-drive-over tone.

I turn to face Ed. He is dressed in what I call the Buick Cutlass Sedan—an oversized, greyish, shiny silver suit. The blazer's bulky shoulder padding splays off his shoulders, and the two-sizes-too-large pleated pants sag like a droopy diaper. I'm trying to maintain eye contact, but the bulging and puffing ripples of his ill-fitting blue dress shirt shift as he moves. Thankfully, there is a saving grace—a nice tie. It's vivid blue and highlights his hazel eyes.

"So what brings you to BNI?," Ed's jovial voice continues. "Steve invited me," I share, trying to shake the last vestiges of the dream world that is calling me back to a snuggly slumber. I'm about to start rolling around and nuzzling the air when Ed's voice yanks me back, "So what is it that you do?" Oh yeah, that's why I'm here. "Uh, I dress men," I hurriedly say, realizing I have to answer this man's question snappily or seem like I accidently stumbled in thinking this was a prework sobriety meetup.

"What does that mean?" Ed asks. "Sorry," I reply, trying to enunciate, "In my awake state I create wardrobes for men based on their lifestyle, goals, and budget." As if seeing a unicorn, Ed gingerly but firmly hands me his card, and urgency spills into his tone. "Please call," he says.

"You got it," I respond, just as the clink of "please take your seats" takes over the room. "Heck, this networking thing is a breeze," I think, as I pull out a chair from the U-shaped table set-up. "But there's no damn way I'm getting up this early to attend one of these things again."

At 2:00 p.m., (a more humane time of day), I'm dialing Ed as promised. "So, tell me what your goals are?" I ask. "To be honest," Ed says, "I haven't thought about that exactly. I just know that things could be better, and I have this sense that I would get taken more seriously if I dressed better. But I don't know what better means. When I go shopping, I'm not sure what fits me and is right for what I do. I'm an independent patent agent, so not only am I responsible for getting new business, but my clients have to trust me enough to divulge very sensitive information about intellectual property. Also, I want to start doing more public speaking and have no idea what to wear for that."

"Who are the people you are meeting with at client sites?" I ask. "So that's the thing," Ed replies. "I meet with product managers and senior management and have to gain their trust, and I know a couple of the companies I do work with have more that they could outsource to me, but I haven't been able to, so to speak, get it out of them."

"Part of my other challenge is that I work from home, so it's not like I need to wear suits every day. That being said, I'd like to be wearing something that isn't horrifying when I work at a coffee shop or run errands."

Ed's plight was and is the quintessential entrepreneur challenge. Unlike someone with a more predictable day gig and schedule of responsibilities, an entrepreneur's activities vary widely. Ed needed a much smaller assortment of business wear since he dressed up for meetings and events a few times a week, while at least 50 percent of his schedule only required that he look "not homeless." (I once had a tech entrepreneur client tell me that before he started working with me, he feared taking his coffee on the train because people tried to give him money.)

About a week after our phone call, when I opened Ed's closet for the wardrobe review, I saw a very familiar situation. He had a lot of clothes, none of which he enjoyed wearing. He was trapped in the same three options: a suit, blue shirt and khakis, or Dad jeans and polo. Looking at what Ed had to choose from, it was no surprise that he did not feel completely confident in social settings.

Clothing that fit in the dressy casual or casual chic category was completely missing from his wardrobe.

After our shopping and styling session, during which we selected 12 core pieces that could easily be interchanged to create a week-plus of looks for his full range of business and weekend activities, Ed would periodically get in touch to share all the positive feedback he was getting on his new clothes and style. He then began hiring me yearly to refresh and add as needed, and every year he seemed to be getting better and better in all areas. Business was booming, and he was dating someone he had been coveting since their first chance meeting—a friend's neighbor who loved going on bike rides in her bikini. Although she had always made him nervous, with his newfound confidence they were starting to spend time together.

Flash forward two more years to 2012. Ed has moved to California with his bikini-biking girlfriend and is successfully continuing his practice out there and chatting with Bloomberg about working with me:

One client, Ed Kelley, 57, a Redwood City, California-based patent agent, knew he needed a change but wasn't sure what that change should be. After meeting Sorokin, he tossed out his old clothes, which included billowy dress shirts and baggy khakis, and replaced them with trim fit button-down shirts and casual twill pants. Comfy sneakers were out, slip-on moccasins were in. One reason for the wardrobe redo: Kelley had started to do more public speaking and needed to look more authoritative and have more confidence. The makeover worked: "I felt I was a together guy," says Kelley. "I got bigger clients and doubled my income."

During that networking breakfast many years before, Ed absolutely would not have predicted such a conclusion. The clothes you choose are the keys to the kingdom, though, and I'm going to make that accessible to you.

THE 4 MYTHS OF DRESSING WELL

It's not just that shopping is a Sharknado of overwhelming options and uncertainty that keeps good men trapped in their dorky shadow selves. There are also some core beliefs that consciously or subconsciously stand squarely in the way of taking style and confidence to the next level with ease.

Myth #1. You've gotta dress fancier/flashier/not like yourself. BS. Say it with me, dressing well does not mean dressing up. You don't need fancy clothes. You need great-fitting, quality basics that make you feel like a rock star every day.

Myth #2. It's gonna be uncomfortable. *Au contraire mon frère*. Being completely comfortable is a huge part of good style. This isn't women's fashion, so we'll be having no suffering for beauty thank you.

Myth #3. It's gonna be expensive. Chances are you've been spending your money in the wrong places. Yes, quality costs more, but it's way better to spend a bit more on a few well-made, versatile pieces that you'll love rotating through than it is to have a closet full of clothes you got on sale with nothing you really want to wear.

Myth #4. It's hard/too much effort. It takes no more effort to put on great-fitting, comfortable shirts and denim than it does to put on their dumpy counterparts. I'm going to show you the simple formula behind good style.

WHAT'S IN THIS BOOK & HOW TO GET AWESOMENESS OUT OF IT

This book is split into three sections for ease of tasty consumption as you put the myths of dressing well behind you and arm yourself for sartorial success.

First, you will learn my secret Style 4Mula, which breaks down the DNA of good style and allows you to nail the perfect look for any situation in four steps. Anytime you see someone who looks great, whether in the most casual setting or at a black tie event, it's because all four of these principles are in play. If they don't look good, that means one or more elements of the Style 4Mula are missing.

Second, you will find 30 days of head-to-toe business casual looks. These looks, which include styles that are appropriate for workplaces ranging from tech startups to law firms, will also come with directions on how to dress them up, dress them down, or make them edgier, giving you 120 outfit combination ideas from which to choose. In addition to rocking it out Monday-Friday, each of these looks will also have recommendations for the type of activity it would be appropriate for, including interviews, pitch meetings, your TED Talk, etc.

Third, I will delve more deeply into the realm of one of those activities—the interview—and break down what to wear to an interview when a suit and tie won't fly.

Lastly, be forewarned that this guide is littered with F-words (fashion terminology). However, the book is also chock full of visuals, and if you get lost there's a handy glossary starting on page 137 that you can reference for assistance. By the end of your journey through this book you'll be a pro, so fear not!

As for the awesomeness, the best way to get all of it out of this book is to read it repeatedly. Then talk about it. And think about it. And tweet about it. And talk about it some more. And visualize it. And study the looks. And adopt parts of the looks. Or the whole looks. Or email me to help you.

THE STYLE
4MULA

Having the
right look
for any
occasion
means
getting only
four things
right.

THE STYLE 4MULA CRASH COURSE

Applied knowledge is power. When physicists started quantifying the principles behind how the universe works, they could apply those formulas to a variety of earthly situations to achieve amazing and unprecedented progress. So shall you, my friend, make leaps and bounds with the knowledge in this book.

In my style lab, I have spent years distilling a formula to find the perfect look for any occasion in just four steps. Gentlemen, I present to you, the Style 4Mula. This formula is the science behind style, and it allows you to blend the ease of the codified suiting formula with the versatility to thrive across the full spectrum of activities and levels of formality.

I'll delve more deeply into all four of these principles in a moment. As with science, however, you can get way too deep and granular, so I have edited down the most usable examples in each category to avoid overwhelming you and to give you the easiest amount of info that will have the biggest impact.

What's that you say? Scrap the boring list method and introduce the elements of the Style 4Mula in haiku form so they'll be easier to remember? Well okay, but only because you asked.

Fitting, feeling right,
Layers and accessories—
The Style 4Mula

Well that probably didn't clear anything up, so here's a handy chart summarizing the Style 4Mula. Again, with this know-how you can put yourself together right for any situation. Liquid gold, people!

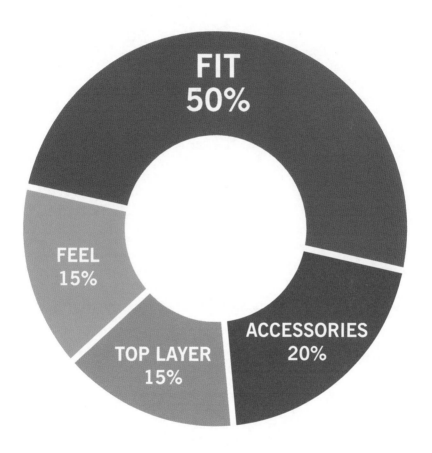

PART 1
FIT

The foundation
of good style.
Without
nailing the fit,
no matter
how nice
or expensive
the garment is,
you won't
look good.

THE STYLE 4MULA: FIT

Men can have a very difficult time assessing what fits them, so let's distill the principle of good fit to its essence; that way, like a great vodka, it will be easier to consume.

How a garment fits you is determined by how well its size and its cut work with your current body shape, weight, and height. Garments of the same size can have different cuts; that is, they can be shaped and proportioned differently to work with different body types. Regardless of your body type, however, your main goals are to emphasize strong, broad shoulders and to narrow your waist. As a man you always want to create a V with your torso.

The suit may have gone but the goal of emphasizing your V shape has not, my friend.

It may sound old fashioned, but just like the hourglass silhouette is thought of as female, the V is thought of as male. It's evolutionary psychology; both women and men want to see strong shoulders on a man. Back in the day, it meant you could take down a saber-toothed tiger and protect against enemies. Today, it still denotes power and strength. So if you only take one thing away from this book, it's that when it comes to how your clothes fit and what you wear, your goal is always to be accentuating your torso into the V shape. (Don't worry if you're not naturally shaped that way. Well-chosen pieces can help create that silhouette.)

Now that we have the goal for your shape, on to your goal for fit.

FIT BY DECADE

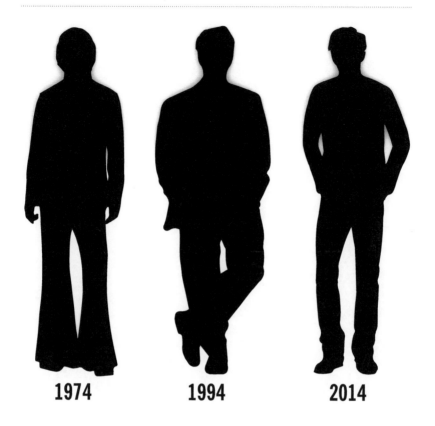

1974 **1994** **2014**

Those of you who didn't have Facebook in high school may remember a time when Vanilla Ice was paving the way for future, ornately-dressed white rappers, and it looked cool to be wearing anything puffy.

Silhouettes change with the times, though, so don't get trapped in time like a fossil. Imagine if you didn't update since the steam engine? (Simmer down steampunks.) Not updating since the last decade is just as hazardous, because you're communicating in a non-verbal way that you've lost relevancy.

The key to looking current is understanding what the fit silhouette of the day is. Currently, and for the foreseeable future (fashion gods do not smite me for this declaration), it is about closely framing and flattering your natural form. This means your natural shoulders, rather than the big shoulders of the 80s and 90s.

QUICK-'N'-NOT-SO-DIRTY FIT GUIDE

Up Top, Good Fit Starts At Your Shoulders

Here's a fit rule of thumb: when you put a shirt on, check to make sure the shoulder seams do not droop past the curve of your shoulder. The fabric by your ribcage should skim along your body, gliding down to shape your torso, with no fabric pulling because it's too tight or billowing away because it's too loose. Of those, the too-puffy shirt is much more prevalent.

The man shapes below are the same size, but the dude on the right looks dumpy instead of masculine. Make sure your shirts' shoulder seams aren't killing your V. They say all the world's a stage, but that doesn't mean you need to be wearing the curtain.

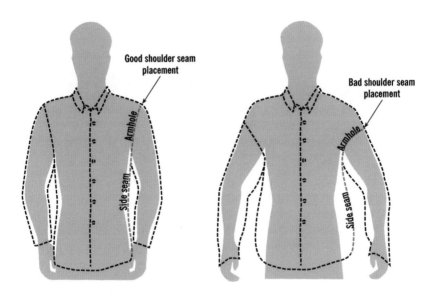

Good shoulder seam placement

Bad shoulder seam placement

Below The Belt:

Pants also come in different cuts for a variety of backsides and thighs. Fit wise, your pants must be in a shape so the fabric is skimming your legs and tuckus without an excess of fabric. You don't want them sadly drooping off your backside, and they have to be the right length.

If you need a belt to keep your pants up, they are too big. The belt may hoist your pants up a little, but it can't fix the fit in the rest of the leg, and compressing extra fabric around the waist creates a diapering effect. Even on the E*TRADE baby, diapers do not come across as professional.

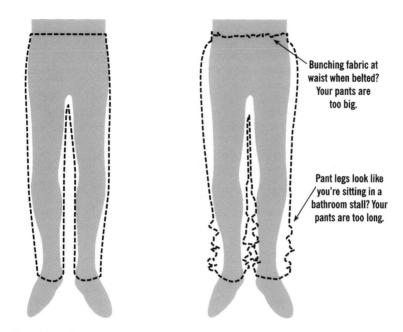

Bunching fabric at waist when belted? Your pants are too big.

Pant legs look like you're sitting in a bathroom stall? Your pants are too long.

Breaking Good:

"Break" is the term for the folds or bends that appear in the lower leg of your pants when you wear them. Your pants will have more or less break depending on how much longer the pant leg is than your actual leg. To help you nail the fit below the belt, the illustration below shows how different types of pants have different "acceptable" amounts of break. For example, if you had as much break in your slacks as you would with casual denim, you'd look like you were drowning in your big brother's pants. Personal preference also comes into play; in general, when you're going for a more formal or neat look, you want a smaller amount of break.

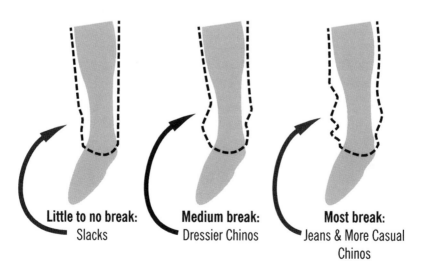

Little to no break:
Slacks

Medium break:
Dressier Chinos

Most break:
Jeans & More Casual
Chinos

Size:

Trust no one. The X-Files tagline applies equally to government agencies and fashion retailers. Vanity sizing, variations by designer, the lack of universal sizing standards, and production inconsistencies within a single brand mean you can never rely on the size label. So, don't follow labels like the North Star or you'll be led astray. Instead, when you're trying something on in the store, pay attention to how each garment feels and rests on your body and not what the label says. You know how sometimes when a fighter is training, his sensei puts a blindfold on him so he can "see" what is happening without his vision? Finding the right size should be kinda like that, except no one is gonna thump the back of your knees with a bamboo sword as you're trying on clothes.

For all your garments, after size, the cut will influence how the fabric forms around your body.

Cut:

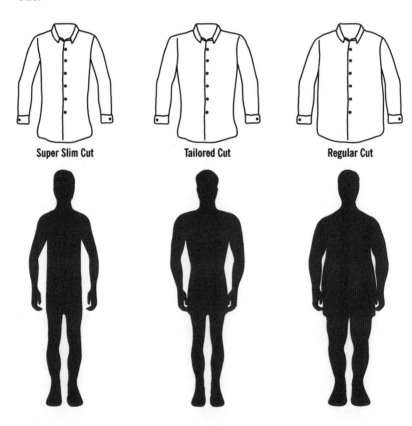

Super Slim Cut   **Tailored Cut**   **Regular Cut**

This is often the first stumbling block. Every brand cuts for a particular body type—the men perceived as the target clients. If you buy a shirt that's the wrong cut for you, even if it's the right size, it won't fit you. WTF? you ask. Size and cut are different factors, and they both determine fit. For example, without even looking in the mirror, if the fit is right in the shoulders but you can grab a handful of fabric on either side of your shirt and not change how the buttons are fitting around your chest, then you're wearing the wrong cut and there's too much fabric around your midsection.

Fit fails can be avoided by choosing the right size and cut, and having any needed adjustments made by a tailor.

Some guys have an easy time finding clothes right off the rack that fit perfectly. The next section is for the other 85% of the male population.

Have a Hard Time Finding Clothes That Fit? Try This.

Most times men end up settling in what they wear because it's incredibly time consuming to find the right fit in a garment, let alone coordinate a whole look of great-fitting pieces. Whether you're the kind of guy who finds himself swimming in most shirts, who can't get pants that don't sag in the back, or who can never find sleeves that are long enough, it's easy to feel hopeless when it seems that nothing out there is really right for you. But behold, there's a double rainbow and lots of gold awaiting when you know where to look.

Where, in general, should you begin? First, know that the cut that best flatters you depends on your body's current shape. If you don't have an off-the-rack body, educate yourself on different brands and hone in on ones that are best cut for you.

Boutiques, European brands, and youth-focused retailers typically carry very lean cuts, while national box retailers have a wide variety of cuts that typically include a bigger selection of larger sizes.

Also know that brands are recognizing the decookiecutterification (totally rocked that one in Words With Friends) of America, and most now offer several cuts to choose from in both shirts and pants. So unless you're an octopus, you should be able to find something that's within alteration range of a perfect fit. Hazzah!

If you don't mind interfacing with other humans, ask the store managers of the shops that sell clothes that seem in line with your lifestyle and budget which of the brands they carry will best fit your body. If they don't carry anything, but you like their aesthetic (the look), make your case heard. Write to corporate, and tell them you've got money to burn and can't find what you would buy there. If women got themselves the right to vote, you can get your local clothing retailer to carry pants that fit.

If you're the shy type, you can also try out how different brands and cuts fit you without ever leaving your house or amassing a campaign. Find clothes online at retailers with free shipping (both ways) so you can mail back anything that isn't right. You can also chat with their customer support online about the merchandise.

(Just remember that with both in-store and online "styling help," that person's job is to sell merchandise rather than look out for what's best for you. So it's incredibly important to listen to your spidey senses. When you try on the clothes, if you're not feelin' it for any reason, no matter how much the salesperson or store stylist insists they love it on you, do not buy or wear it!)

After trying out a few brands to see what fits you best, find a good tailor to help tweak the clothes you buy. Do so with an internet search in your area. (Yelp was created as more than just an outlet for people to provide their personal reflection on every single aspect of their meal.) If that doesn't work, go to the highest-end retailer in your area, or near your workplace, and ask them to whom they send their alterations. Chances are the tailor they trust to take in the Gucci will do a brilliant job reattaching the original hem to your denim after they've been altered to your perfect length.

Also, know what the easy fixes are: tailoring sleeves and pant bottoms to your correct length makes the difference between looking like your clothes were made for you and looking like you're wearing hand-me-downs. Since pants are easier to take in and shorten up, if something fits great in the booty but is too long, buy the pants and pay the extra $10-$25 (depending on where you live) to have them altered. It's usually more difficult to take a garment out (make it bigger), because it might not have enough fabric in the seams to do so.

Another option is to go custom: there is simply no feeling like wearing clothing that was literally made for you. Custom clothiers are more prevalent today than ever before (thank Harvard Business School), and custom prices have come down and will often beat off-the-rack prices. Custom prices are based on the fabric you select, but a custom button-down shirt can start at $100, whereas a designer, off-the-rack shirt starts at $150. Custom is not instant gratification though, as it takes 3-6 weeks depending on your order. If you want to give the custom route a try make sure to do your research; find a place that doesn't have a large minimum order and that has a clear and fair return policy.

Finally, you can eliminate the chore and uncertainty of it all by hiring an experienced wardrobe stylist; a good independent fashion stylist (not a shill for stores) will be able to find you complete outfits that fit you well in less time than it will take you to find a new shirt.

PART 2
FEEL

Every garment
sets a different
tone and reveals
something about
your personality.
Your clothes
should feel right
for both who you
are and what
you are doing.

THE STYLE 4MULA: FEEL
Four Flavors of Business Casual

One of the compounding difficulty factors of nailing the right look for work is that the standard for "business casual" looks different from office to office and from job to job. Over the years of working with individual clients and corporations, though, I've realized that business casual can be broken down into four flavors. It's important to identify which sandbox either you or your clients are playing in; good style depends upon context. The goal is always to look capable and "appropriately professional" for the setting, and that depends on the level of formality of your job, your industry, and your activities. Let's sample these four flavors now.

EXECUTIVE CASUAL

The most formal of the bunch. Executive casual spans from a suit without the tie to slacks with a dress shirt and a blazer, and occasionally chinos or dress denim can be appropriate.

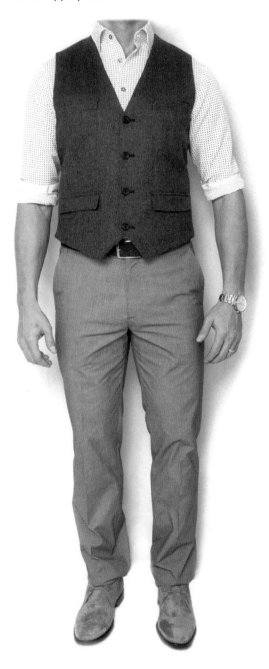

CLASSIC BUSINESS CASUAL

Classic business casual is the most common form of business wear seen across offices in America. The range includes traditional pairings of sport coats with chinos and button-down shirts on the dressy end. In the middle of the range are sweaters and chinos, and the relaxed end consists of denim with casual button-downs or polos.

CREATIVE CASUAL

Creative casual is similar to classic business casual in terms of the range but is typically more fashion forward with a lot of designer denim. There's an acceptance of fabrics, finishes, and cuts in the clothing and accessories that are on trend and very "now" that could be considered a little too non-traditional in classic business casual.

TECH CASUAL

More so than in any other business casual flavor, comfort and utility rule the domain of tech casual. The range here includes all types of denim with untucked button-downs or T-shirts, and on the dressier end are chinos and any shirt with a collar.

FINDING THE RIGHT FEEL FOR YOU

Once you figure out what flavor of business casual you're going with, your next challenge is to personalize your looks to bring out your individual style. When I have a consultation call, my clients usually say something like, "I don't want to look flashy," or, "I don't want to look like the typical finance guy." That's all controlled by the feel of the garments they choose.

So what gives a garment its feel? The biggest influencing factors are fabric and construction. For example, a navy pinstripe wool blazer and a brown corduroy blazer with elbow patches say very different things about your personality and what you do. When you look at clothes, start paying attention to the fabric's fiber, color, pattern, and any construction details like zippers, contrast stitching, or other embellishments. These are the design details that communicate the most to the world about your personality.

I was giving a talk once about incorporating personal style into your business wear, and a gentleman in the audience proudly displayed the lime green mock turtleneck he had worn to jazz up his outfit. His neon half neck was sticking out of a giant blue dress shirt that was unbuttoned to the middle of his chest, and he was sporting oversized, black-pleated, droopy polyester pants. In his mind, adding the Emeril "Bam!" of bright green into his wardrobe communicated that he was different. And it did, but not in the way he was intending.

At the core of it, he didn't have the right ingredients. As I learned from my 13-year experiment with vegetarianism, there's no way to put portobello mushroom caps on the grill and expect to bite into a burger. In the same way, there was no way he was coming off as the "cool, different guy" by combining old traditional business cuts and fabrics with a neon ski top. Our friend would have achieved his desired goal much more effectively if he'd chosen a casual tailored button-down with a subtle print and if he'd swapped out his pants for a form-fitting color chino.

Although his attempt was unsuccessful, Mr. Neon Ski Top did have one thing going for him. He had thought about how he wanted to come across. Most men have yet to identify their own style in this new business casual world, but I notice that most want to strive to look effortless and to avoid looking flashy. Once they give it thought beyond that, they usually want some combination of the following descriptors, in order of popularity:

- Confident
- Professional
- Capable
- Approachable
- Sharp
- Pulled together
- A little edgy
- Creative
- Like the guy in charge
- Someone who has his s@#* together
- Stylish
- Well-traveled

In order to feel more confident in your clothes or get pieces that "feel more like you," think about the impression you want to give when people look at you. When you try on clothes, focus in on how they make you feel when you're looking at yourself. Do they make you feel good and do they evoke the experience that you want? If not, they're not right for you.

Some other factors you should consider when trying to get the right feel are:

Dressing in Context: Out-of-context items usually take the form of activewear or mountain wear. You wouldn't wear a business shoe to the gym, so don't wear athletic sneakers to work. If you're aiming for casual and comfortable footwear, there are many options out there, including casual sneakers, that will look appropriate and feel good. Similarly, a North Face fleece—and that's the "good" fleece—over business clothes is a no-no, because sport gear mixed with traditional business attire irreparably ruins your swagger. A bulbous fleece reinforces the orb, whereas a well-cut casual jacket reinforces the V. Casual jackets that work brilliantly at the office are easy to find and are constructed to be form-flattering. We want comfy, but also in the shape of a man, not a blueberry.

Dressing Near Your Age: It's sad to see a 40-year-old wearing a T-shirt with skulls and dragons on it, but just as sad is the 20-year-old dressing in pleated khakis and a boxy blue blazer. Neither of them accomplishes what he wants—to look younger or more mature, respectively. Younger guys can get away with bolder and trendier choices; men with a few more years behind them should opt for more classic pieces in modern cuts and fabrics.

Dressing Beneath Your Paygrade: The mangled triangle of a white Hanes T-shirt poking out of your button-down, aka the underachiever's ascot, is a perfect example of dressing beneath your paygrade. Unless Best Buy is regulating your attire, we want clean neck lines.

Wearing Colors That Work For You: There are a lot of resources out there for finding colors that go with your skin tone. As a general rule of thumb, the lighter your skin tone and hair, the lighter the shades of any color you want to wear. For example, a light-skinned blond would be overpowered by a deep burgundy button-down, but would look good in its lighter counterpart—a very light pink. For a non-traditional color scheme suggestion tool, go to https://kuler.adobe.com/create/color-wheel. Choose the colors on the wheel that you think most closely resemble your skin tone and hair color, and then play around with the options. You'll stay within tones that complement your skin, and you may get a bunch of color coordination options you had never considered.

Now that you've become more familiar with the four flavors of business casual, the concept of feel, and some dos and don'ts, let's hone your skills further with a challenge!

FEEL QUIZ

Let's take a quick look at
a few garments and see
which is more appropriate
depending on the feel.

TAUPE SUEDE BOOT **VS.** TWO-TONE BOOT

Which of these feels more appropriate to wear with slacks to a colleague's spring wedding?

Answer: Taupe Suede Boot (A). The light color and simple, elegant lines fit better with spring than the heavier and more rugged, dark brown, thick-soled two-tone boot.

TEAL QUARTER-ZIP SWEATER  VS. FRANKENSTEIN SWEATER

Which of these would feel more appropriate for a 45-year-old, and which for a 25-year-old?

Answer: **The Frankenstein sweater (B)** could be pulled off by a guy in his twenties.

NAVY SUEDE DRIVER VS. GREY PATENT DRIVER

Which of these feels best for a client dinner in Vegas on a Friday night, and which feels better for a networking breakfast?

Answer: The grey patent leather driver (B), with its shinier finish, is more appropriate for the Vegas dinner. The navy suede driver (A) is more subdued and more appropriate for the networking breakfast.

ZIP-FRONT SWEATER **VS.** COLOR-TRIM CARDIGAN

Which of these feels a bit more edgy?

Answer: **The zip-front sweater (A)** has an edgier feel, while the cardigan is a more classic look.

LEATHER-BURNISHED TOE LOAFERS  VS. CROCODILE-FINISH DRIVER

Which of these feels more appropriate for a board meeting in Boston?

Answer: Boston is traditionally more formal in its dress codes than cities on the West Coast, and board meetings are typically more formal events than staff meetings. The classic look of the leather-burnished toe loafers (A) is more appropriate for a Boston board meeting.

BREAKING FREE OF THE CORPORATE UNIFORM

Especially When You Don't Do Your Own Shopping

Are you ready to break free from the corporate uniform and put this tutorial on feel to work? Does your woman dress you and shop for you? Yeah, we can tell. Listen up, if you're one of the men who lays it on his wife to pick out all his clothes (perhaps you've stopped going shopping with her because you think shopping is a horrible life-sucking activity that takes forever, or perhaps it causes some arguments between you and your dove), and you don't wanna keep looking like the typical business guy, go pour yourself two fingers of single malt and hand this over to her with the following page open and a kiss.

If you do your own shopping, proceed with the scotch, but read the next page yourself. Self-sufficiency is a beautiful thing.

Ladies, this excerpt is for you. I realize it might be weird getting a random note from a book your man is reading. I know he's kind of a boor about going shopping for clothes. I know that he may not put in any serious effort himself, or he may label himself as "not a fashion guy" and put his entire image on you. He even may bug you all the time with, "Which should I wear?," and you answer, sunken-hearted, knowing neither option is a good one. But that's all going to change! I swear it, I'm making it super easy for him to understand how to look good. Also remember, you are his first line of defense as you make his clothing choices for him in the store (even if you've been forced into a small selection by his earlier refusals to try anything new).

Without further ado, here are some options to have your man stop looking like a corporate drone. Men have a limited set of garments, so it comes down to switching up the fabrics, colors, prints, and patterns to other work-appropriate options.

Five simple ways to break your man out of a blue-shirt-and-khaki uniform:

→ Diversify his khakis by incorporating additional colors like tobacco, olive, or dark burgundy chinos. They'll all go just as brilliantly with the blue and white shirts in his closet now.

→ Ease up on plain, solid-colored dress shirts and add a few pattern button-downs. Prints and patterns with multiple colors, at least one of which coordinates with the pant or top layer, make the outfit appear effortlessly pulled together.

→ Add a tailored vest. A vest is a perfect in-between garment because it has a softer feel than a blazer but means business more than a sweater. Vests can be worn year-round and go with slacks, chinos, or denim.

⟳ Add a pocket square. Get an assortment of color and print ones. A thin sliver showing from a sport coat or vest looks refined, is completely business appropriate, and is a refreshing alternative to a tie.

⟳ Plain black and brown belts = snoozefest. Switch up the belt color, material, and texture.

⟳ Lastly, please NEVER EVER EVER buy him pleated khaki pants or Dad jeans. We've all suffered enough.

Thank you, ladies! Your significant other may now resume reading this book. Please ignore it if he's drinking scotch early in the day. I swear I'm a good influence.

PART 3
TOP
LAYER

A well-chosen
finishing layer
on top
elevates your
look, creates
character and
depth, and helps
reinforce the
masculine
V silhouette.

THE STYLE 4MULA: TOP LAYER

Most men think of a look or outfit in twos (a top and a bottom), but with layering—just like a ménage à trois—three is better.

Where the feel of a garment shows your personality, layering is where you get your individuality. Every guy has a blue shirt, but it's what he wears with that blue shirt that sets him apart. In addition to adding character, the top layers elevate your look, reinforce masculine lines, and can be a place to hold your phone and wallet.

This doesn't mean you need to stuff yourself into a suit jacket. When it comes to business casual, adding a top finishing piece can class you up, whether it's a cashmere hoodie, a tailored vest, a casual sport coat, or a lightweight jacket. Which of those options is the best fit for you depends on the culture of your workplace and clients.

A well-chosen top layer can also do wonders for reinforcing the V. Remember those gents who had trouble getting clothes that fit and looked good? For a man with a larger midsection, a tailored vest slims the torso. For a lean guy, a heavier-weight slim-cut sweater or hoodie adds a bit more visual heft to the silhouette.

If you are a guy whose body temperature runs high (you sweat through everything), you can omit the top layer or employ vests, which allow your underarm sweat factories to remain uncovered. But if you omit the top layer, you have to make sure the other elements in the formula are on point, with choice accessories and great-fitting pieces that have just the right feel.

Top-Layer Options: If you have at least one option in each of these categories, you should pretty much be set for any business casual situation.

Sport Coats and Blazers

They come in every fabric and color and can range from being completely casual to dressy. They are also great for carrying your wallet, keys, and phone, even if the jacket spends most of the day on the back of your chair.

Vests

Vests come in tailored and knit varieties. Casual vests pair handsomely with slacks, chinos, or denim. They are good over dress shirts, casual button-downs, or henleys (cotton crew-neck shirts with a button closure at the top). A vest can take your look up a notch but is more relaxed than a sport coat or blazer. If you don't enjoy wearing jackets, a vest would be a great top-layering piece for you.

Sweaters

Most men hate sweaters because they remember being stuffed into itchy bags of wool as children. The key is to get the right thickness and yarn. Cashmere is going to be the softest; cashmere blends should also work. You never want to get anything even remotely itchy because you won't wear it even if you really like the color. You also want to get something that is thin enough so you can layer it underneath a jacket, but not so thin that when you wear a button-down underneath it the buttons show through the sweater fabric.

Lightweight Jackets

Unlined lightweight jackets that can be worn indoors come in a variety of cuts—from motorcycle to safari—and they can make a great casual substitute for a sport coat or blazer.

PART 4

ACCESSORIES

Your
not-so-secret
weapons that tie
your whole look
together and
make you legend

THE STYLE 4MULA: ACCESSORIES
Meet Mark

Mark hired me because although he thought his style was "okay" and he could "get by" with it, he wanted to up his game at work. Mark's law firm has a classic business casual policy, but his boss's boss was quite the style afficionado, and Mark was a believer in "dress for the job you want, not the one you have." (Which reminds me, I need to go pick up my astronaut suit from the cleaners—ketchup stain, ugh.)

During our consultation, Mark told me, as many men do, that he wasn't sure what kind of accessories were appropriate (or even what types of accessories there were, beyond belts and shoes). However, he also felt that accessories "would be my thing if I knew what I was doing."

At our shopping session, I focused on getting Mark core pieces that he would rotate throughout the week, along with a good number of distinctive accessories. For our purposes, we are defining "distinctive" as having quality materials, good construction, and subtle design details. (Really loud and in-your-face accessories do more harm than good.)

The following week I got a very excited email from Mark. Apparently, in a crowded elevator, the boss's boss—who rarely hobnobbed with the junior staff—could not resist from commenting on Mark's antique lapel pin that I had picked out for him. They struck up a conversation about it, and as they walked down the hall, leaving Mark's peers behind him, the boss's boss also started noticing Mark's belt along with his shoes and colored shoelaces. Mark was thrilled that his boss's boss not only noticed him, but looked on him as a kindred spirit ("He invited me to play in their executive squash game!"). Yep, while bonding over accessories, Mark and his boss's boss became BFFs (best fashion friends). You can't bribe your way into face time like that (unless you're in Congress), but well-chosen accessories got the job done.

Accessories tie your look together with a gorgeous gift ribbon and give it just the right amount of zest. So it's time we move beyond the reversible belt and black and brown shoes. Accessories are where you can express yourself further. Play with color, leather finishes, metals, shapes, etc., and if expressing yourself doesn't fire you up, keep in mind that accessories can cut your social efforts by at least half. Why? Because they start conversations.

There's a lot to choose from in the realm of accessories, so much so in fact that it can be overwhelming for a guy to figure out what to do with what.

So I wrote you a poem about all the items available for your business casual pleasure. Very loosely based on the great Dr. Seuss classic, "Oh, the Places You'll Go!," (my hands are clean, Trademark Commission!), I present to you...

OH, THE ACCESSORIES YOU'LL KNOW!

You have brains in your head. But feet in bad shoes. Not sure which accessories to choose. You're on your own no more.

Let's start with the head, too often ignored.
With so many options, you'll never be bored.

There are hats for all seasons, all head shapes and sizes.
You must feel confident in it to wear it, this stylist advises.

Eyewear and sunnies frame your beautiful mug;
Don't settle for gas station sunglasses, you lug.

Scarves are not just for winter, choose the right weight and size;
With a spring jacket or blazer, they can highlight your eyes.

And do not be afraid when the cold weather shoves;
Keep your hands from the chill with a nice pair of gloves.

To your lapel, add a sparkle of silver or gold;
Pins come in designs that are both new and old.

If you like to have something encircling your wrist,
Wear a watch, cuff or bracelet, you get the gist.

Most men rarely wear ties and that is all right,
But narrow knit or wool ties are not quite so uptight.

While cufflinks can often add class to your jacket,
A well-chosen tie pin puts you in a new style bracket.

Pocket squares add elegance, but needn't stick out completely;
Your pocket should show a mere sliver discreetly.

Suspenders and bow ties can set you apart,
But you have to avoid looking like an old fart.

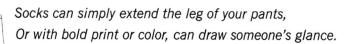

The belts and the shoes are so often ignored;
Go beyond black and brown and you shall be adored.

Lots of comfortable footwear has the proper aesthetic,
Lace-ups, slip-ons, boots and sneakers (if they aren't athletic).

Socks can simply extend the leg of your pants,
Or with bold print or color, can draw someone's glance.

And please don't forget, you can change your shoelaces;
Switch up the color, and you're off to the races.

Class up the places where you hold your stuff;
Your wallet and bag have to be up to snuff.

Skivvies of course are a personal choice,
But performance fabric boxer briefs might make you rejoice.

Find your finishing touches and wear them with pride;
Any uncertainty ruins the ride.

THE **30** LOOKS

N ow that we've discussed all of the fundamentals of the Style 4Mula, get ready for a visual inspiration buffet. Along with each of the next 30 outfits, I give you ideas on how you can dress it up, dress it down, or make it edgier. That means that in this next section there are 120 outfit ideas. You're welcome, America. Also, for each look, I give you the range of business activities that it would be appropriate for, as well as a quick reference visual combination code for each look.

Keep in mind that you don't need to duplicate these looks exactly; I've styled them for you as a base formula. If you're not the type of dude to rock out a color chino, that's okay; now that we've had that whole chat about the feel of a garment, you know enough to switch something out and personalize the look so it will feel more "you." Don't like shawl cardigans? Swap that piece out with a zip-front sweater or lightweight jacket instead. You might take just a couple of elements that inspire you, or you can use the whole look. I've chosen modern colors that go beyond basic blue yet will coordinate just as easily with the colors you are used to wearing. Freaked out by color denim? Go with a classic blue in your rendition. You get the idea, now get in there and get stylin'!

WEAR FOR:

- ➡ Client pitch meetings
- ➡ Presentations
- ➡ Work to date nights
- ➡ Meeting with the bank

DRESS IT UP
Switch out the jeans for a pair of grey wool slacks.

DRESS IT DOWN
Remove the vest and replace the boots with a pair of loafers.

EDGE IT UP
Wear a leather jacket instead of the blazer.

LOOK ❶ COMPONENTS

TOP LAYERS

BLACK & GREY MICRO-CHECK BLAZER

BURGUNDY KNIT VEST

WHITE HENLEY

PANT

DARK WASH JEAN

ACCESSORIES

BLACK CAP-TOE BOOT

TWO-TONE DRESS BELT

SOCKS

WEAR FOR:

- → Tech meetups
- → Entrepreneur events
- → Trade shows
- → Informal interviews

@AskEmmi TIP | Grey shoes go with any color pants, which make them way more versatile than their traditional black and brown counterparts.

 ### DRESS IT UP
Add a dress shirt underneath the sweater and swap out the loafer for a wingtip shoe.

DRESS IT DOWN
Replace the suede loafer with a canvas slip-on and switch to a fabric strap watch.

EDGE IT UP
Swap the loafer for a two-tone boot.

LOOK ❷ COMPONENTS

TOP LAYERS

 LIGHT BLUE V-NECK SWEATER

 NAVY CREW-NECK T-SHIRT

PANT

 GREY WASH DENIM

ACCESSORIES

 GREY LOAFER

 BLUE LEATHER BELT

 SOCKS

WEAR FOR:

→ Keynotes

→ Sales meetings

→ Semi-formal board meetings

→ Interviews that call for professional but not formal suit attire

DRESS IT UP

Add a pocket square or tie and roll down the sleeves.

DRESS IT DOWN

Lose the vest (not literally please).

EDGE IT UP

Switch pant over to a color chino with dark shoes.

LOOK ❸ COMPONENTS

TOP LAYERS

 GREY TAILORED VEST

 RED-DOT PRINT DRESS SHIRT

PANT

 LIGHT GREY SLACK

ACCESSORIES

 TAUPE SUEDE BOOT

 BURGUNDY SUEDE BELT

 SOCKS

WEAR FOR:

- Creative interviews
- Back-my-candidate meetings
- New guard meets the old guard sit-down
- Anytime you want to exude authority without looking stiff

@AskEmmi TIP | A blazer that is made out of jersey fabric has a more casual feel than wool. It looks just as professional with chinos or denim but sets a relaxed tone.

DRESS IT UP

Switch to a French-cuff dress shirt with cufflinks and add a pocket square to the blazer.

DRESS IT DOWN

Remove blazer. Unbutton top buttons and loosen tie an inch. Roll sleeves.

EDGE IT UP

Replace suede boot with a patent leather or bold color shoe.

LOOK ❹ COMPONENTS

TOP LAYERS

JERSEY FABRIC BLAZER

MICRO-DOT DRESS SHIRT

BLACK & WHITE NARROW-DOT WOOL TIE

PANT

NAVY CHINO

ACCESSORIES

NAVY SUEDE BOOTS

SOCKS

WEAR FOR:

- Casual networking events
- Startup meetups
- Field research
- Coffice days

@AskEmmi TIP | A straight-leg chino can be worn over the boot with it fully laced, or with the hem loosely tucked inside the boot with it half unlaced. Note that pant-in-boot is not for the faint of heart, the older crowd, or the traditional workplace.

 DRESS IT UP
Add a print button-down underneath the jacket.

 DRESS IT DOWN
Swap the boots out for loafers.

 EDGE IT UP
Toss on a stitched leather belt and a graphic T-shirt.

LOOK ❺ COMPONENTS

TOP LAYERS

 BLUE COTTON CANVAS MOTORCYCLE JACKET

 WHITE HENLEY

PANT

 DARK BURGUNDY CHINO

ACCESSORIES

 BROWN WINGTIP BOOT

 BROWN LEATHER BELT

 SOCKS

WEAR FOR:

- Client design sessions
- Casual networking events
- Casual staff/status meetings
- Networking booze cruise

DRESS IT UP
Add a sport coat.

 DRESS IT DOWN
Go for light blue denim instead of the khaki color.

 EDGE IT UP
Swap in a camo pant and leather shoe or casual sneaker.

LOOK ❻ COMPONENTS

TOP LAYERS

 LIGHT
GREY
V-NECK
SWEATER

 WHITE
CREW-NECK
T-SHIRT

PANT

 KHAKI
DENIM

ACCESSORIES

 NAVY CANVAS
STRIPE-SOLE SLIP-ON

 MULTI-COLOR
STRIPE FABRIC BELT

SUNGLASSES

WEAR FOR:

- ⟶ SXSW

- ⟶ Vegas nights out done right

- ⟶ Post-convention drinks

- ⟶ Anything after hours

DRESS IT UP
Switch out the polo for a solid-color dress shirt.

DRESS IT DOWN
Replace the polo with a solid-color, tailored T-shirt.

EDGE IT UP
Go for a suede and leather boot instead of the loafer.

LOOK ❼ COMPONENTS

TOP LAYERS

 GREY CONTRAST-COLLAR POLO

PANT

 TONAL-CAMO PRINT DENIM

ACCESSORIES

NAVY SUEDE DRIVER

TWO-TONE BELT

SUNGLASSES

WEAR FOR:

- Casual board meetings
- Informal presentations
- Launch events
- Showings

@AskEmmi TIP | When it comes to blazers, coordination wise, a multi-color check will give you more options and therefore more bang for your wardrobe buck than a solid color.

DRESS IT UP
Wear a tailored vest and button-down or henley underneath the jacket.

DRESS IT DOWN
Go for a sweater instead of the blazer.

EDGE IT UP
Do a black v-neck T-shirt and a studded belt.

LOOK ❽ COMPONENTS

TOP LAYERS

BLACK & GREY MICRO-CHECK BLAZER

ROYAL BLUE V-NECK T-SHIRT

PANT

GREY WASH DENIM

ACCESSORIES

NAVY SUEDE BOOT

STITCHED BROWN LEATHER BELT

SOCKS

WEAR FOR:

- ➔ Half-days
- ➔ Tech events
- ➔ Troubleshooting at client site
- ➔ Internal staff meetings

@AskEmmi TIP | To get the most wear from a sweater, get a lightweight knit that is thick enough to wear a button-down shirt underneath but light enough to be layered underneath a blazer.

 DRESS IT UP
Switch denim to a grey chino.

 DRESS IT DOWN
Switch out boot for a loafer or casual sneaker.

EDGE IT UP
Toss on a leather jacket.

LOOK ❾ COMPONENTS

TOP LAYERS

 PURPLE
ZIP-FRONT
SWEATER

 NAVY
CREW-NECK
T-SHIRT

PANT

 DARK
GREY
DENIM

ACCESSORIES

 TWO-
TONE
BOOT

 BROWN
LEATHER
BELT

 SOCKS

WEAR FOR:

- ➔ Corporate outings
- ➔ Off-site trainings
- ➔ Casual panel discussions
- ➔ Beer tastings

@AskEmmi TIP | Don't be afraid of shoe colors outside of the traditional black and brown. An olive wingtip is seasonless, spices up chinos, and classes up denim.

DRESS IT UP
Switch from a khaki-color pant to a navy chino and add a dark leather shoe.

DRESS IT DOWN
Swap out a polo or henley for the sweater.

EDGE IT UP
Trade in the khaki for a dark grey denim.

LOOK ⑩ COMPONENTS

TOP LAYERS

TWO-TONE
RAGLAN
SLEEVE
SWEATER

PANT

KHAKI
DENIM

ACCESSORIES

OLIVE
LEATHER
WINGTIP

BLACK AND
BROWN
LEATHER
BELT

SOCKS

WEAR FOR:

- ⊘ Glad-you-could-meet-on-
  such-short-notice meetings
- ⊘ Weekend executive
  weekends
- ⊘ Book signings
- ⊘ Business trips

DRESS IT UP
Switch from the woven espadrille to dress shoes and belt.

 DRESS IT DOWN
Remove the pocket square. Switch out the grey chino for a light wash denim.

 EDGE IT UP
Do a darker print button-down and roll the sleeves. Add a lapel pin to the vest. Do a lace-up shoe with contrasting laces.

LOOK ⑪ COMPONENTS

TOP LAYERS

 GREY TAILORED VEST

 BLUE AND BLACK GRID-PATTERN DRESS SHIRT

PANT

 GREY CHINO

ACCESSORIES

 BROWN WOVEN ESPADRILLE SLIP-ONS

 DISTRESSED BROWN LEATHER BELT

 RED AND NAVY PRINT POCKET SQUARE

WEAR FOR:

- → Tech events
- → Impromptu weekend client meetings
- → Working from the coffice
- → Office BBQs

@AskEmmi TIP | A vibrant color driver adds a level of cool to a basic trim sweatshirt and denim.

 DRESS IT UP
Switch hoodie for a shawl collar cardigan or tailored v-neck sweater.

 DRESS IT DOWN
Remove the hoodie and rock the henley.

 EDGE IT UP
Switch out to print sweater and dark shoe.

LOOK ⑫ COMPONENTS

TOP LAYERS

 GREY TEXTURED HOODIE

 WHITE HENLEY

PANT

 DARK WASH DENIM

ACCESSORIES

 ORANGE DRIVER   SOCKS   SUNGLASSES

WEAR FOR:

- Casual speaking events
- Team-building workshops
- Client strategy meetings
- Visits in the field

@AskEmmi TIP | A sweater vest can work when the fit is right. Reinforce the V, not the O. It also depends on what you wear it with; to avoid looking dorky, do not pair with bow tie or boat shoes.

 DRESS IT UP
Switch out to slacks, and change henley to a button-down.

DRESS IT DOWN
Remove the vest and go with a fabric strap watch.

EDGE IT UP
Add a dark henley or T-shirt and a lightweight jacket.

LOOK ⓵③ COMPONENTS

TOP LAYERS

 BURGUNDY KNIT VEST

 WHITE HENLEY

PANT

 DARK WASH DENIM

ACCESSORIES

 BLACK CAP-TOE BOOT

 DRESS BELT

 SOCKS

WEAR FOR:

- → Team meetings
- → Casual company lunches
- → Half-day Fridays
- → Anytime you wanna show how good a T-shirt and chinos can actually look

@AskEmmi TIP | If you're gonna rock a T-shirt by itself, it can't be a box with sleeves like a Hanes undershirt or from a tech conference five years ago. Choose a tailored T-shirt in a quality fabric. A color beyond white seems more intentional or "like an outfit" instead of something you picked up off the floor.

 DRESS IT UP
Add a lightweight print blazer.

 DRESS IT DOWN
Switch out boots for a pair of leather or fabric espadrilles.

EDGE IT UP
Toss on some wrist wear and swap the chinos for dark grey denim.

LOOK ⑭ COMPONENTS

TOP LAYERS
 LIQUID COTTON GREY V-NECK T-SHIRT

PANT
 NAVY CHINO

ACCESSORIES
 NAVY SUEDE BOOT

 BROWN LEATHER BELT

 SOCKS

WEAR FOR:

- ➔ Monday-Friday
- ➔ 14-hour days
- ➔ Upper management
  dressed down
- ➔ Client-site inventories

@AskEmmi TIP | Don't be afraid of colors that sound like they belong on a *My Little Pony* toy. This "light dusted lavender" denim sounds like something not meant for the Y chromosome, but in reality it's a refreshing alternative to khakis and plain blue jeans and goes with just as many colors.

 DRESS IT UP
Replace driver with dress shoes and a vest or sport coat.

DRESS IT DOWN
Switch out the button-down for a tailored T-shirt.

EDGE IT UP
Switch to a boot. Add a knit tie in dark navy or a bold contrast color.

LOOK ⓯ COMPONENTS

TOP LAYERS

 NAVY AND GREY CHECK BUTTON-DOWN

PANT

 LIGHT DUSTED LAVENDER DENIM

ACCESSORIES

 DARK NAVY SUEDE DRIVER

 BROWN LEATHER BELT

 SUNGLASSES

WEAR FOR:

- ➔ Client drinks
- ➔ Off-site meetings
- ➔ Status lunches
- ➔ Tech networking events

DRESS IT UP
Wear a button-down underneath the sweater.

 DRESS IT DOWN
Throw on a pair of light denim.

 EDGE IT UP
Switch from loafer to a motorcycle boot and add a cuff bracelet.

LOOK ⑯ COMPONENTS

TOP LAYERS

 GREY SUEDE TRIM ZIP-FRONT SWEATER

 GREY V-NECK T-SHIRT

PANT

 DARK BURGUNDY CHINO

ACCESSORIES

 DARK NAVY DRIVER

 BROWN LEATHER BELT

 SOCKS

WEAR FOR:

- Strategy meetings
- Pitch sessions
- Client drinks
- Panel discussions

@AskEmmi TIP | Mixing two bold colors can be tricky; increase your chances of success by making one of them an accessory, like shoes or a belt or a pocket square.

DRESS IT UP

Switch out to slacks and a leather loafer or lace-up shoes.

DRESS IT DOWN

Switch loafer to sneaker and white T-shirt underneath.

EDGE IT UP

Go for a pair of coated denim.

LOOK ⑰ COMPONENTS

TOP LAYERS

 TEAL QUARTER-ZIP SWEATER

 GREY V-NECK T-SHIRT

PANT

 LIGHT DUSTED LAVENDER DENIM

ACCESSORIES

 GREEN SUEDE DRIVERS

 BURGUNDY SUEDE BELT

 SOCKS

WEAR FOR:

→ Informal conferences

→ Trade shows

→ Entrepreneur events

DRESS IT UP
Switch belt and shoes to a dark belt and leather shoes and swap T-shirt for a white button-down.

DRESS IT DOWN
Remove hoodie and switch out to a chino and a fabric belt.

EDGE IT UP
Go with a black T-shirt and suede or leather shoe.

LOOK ⑱ COMPONENTS

TOP LAYERS

HEATHERED
GREY HOODIE

ROYAL BLUE
V-NECK
T-SHIRT

PANT

GREY
WASH
DENIM

ACCESSORIES

NAVY CANVAS STRIPE-
SOLE SLIP-ON

DISTRESSED BROWN
LEATHER BELT

WAXED CANVAS BAG

WEAR FOR:

→ Signings

→ Drinks with colleagues

→ Client site visits

→ Anything "after work"

DRESS IT UP
Add a tailored vest over the shirt.

 DRESS IT DOWN
Switch out the dress shirt for a lightweight sweater or henley.

 EDGE IT UP
Switch out to dark grey denim or a two-tone shoe.

LOOK ⑲ COMPONENTS

TOP LAYERS

 BLACK LEATHER JACKET

 RED-DOT PRINT DRESS SHIRT

PANT

 LIGHT GREY SLACKS

ACCESSORIES

 BLACK LEATHER CAP-TOE BOOT

 BURGUNDY SUEDE BELT

 SOCKS

WEAR FOR:

- Casual pitches
- Staff meetings
- Tech events

@AskEmmi TIP | Thin, tonal horizontal stripes are universally flattering in the top layer. High-contrast stripes are good for layering underneath. Wide horizontal stripes only work for men with very lean physiques because they visually widen the body so much.

 DRESS IT UP
Add a grey blazer and a red, orange, or emerald pocket square.

DRESS IT DOWN
Add blue denim and a casual sneaker or loafer.

EDGE IT UP
Wear a wingtip boot or a lighter suede boot.

LOOK ⑳ COMPONENTS

TOP LAYERS

 PURPLE THIN-STRIPE SWEATER

 NAVY CREW-NECK T-SHIRT

PANT

 NAVY CHINO

ACCESSORIES

 NAVY SUEDE BOOT

 BROWN LEATHER BELT

 SOCKS

WEAR FOR:

- Client site visits
- Office hayrides
- Travel days
- Undercover investigative work

@AskEmmi TIP | This look is for the guy who lives in his outdoor vest once fall hits. Puffy vests still have to highlight the shoulders and have a torso-flattering cut.

 DRESS IT UP
Switch out the vest for a grey, navy, or earth-tone blazer and a white linen pocket square.

DRESS IT DOWN
Wear a casual sneaker instead of a loafer.

EDGE IT UP
Do a wingtip boot and some wrist wear.

LOOK ㉑ COMPONENTS

TOP LAYERS

 NAVY NYLON VEST

 BLUE V-NECK SWEATER

 NAVY CREW-NECK T-SHIRT

PANT

 GREY WASH DENIM

ACCESSORIES

 BROWN BURNISHED-TOE LOAFER

 BLUE LEATHER BELT

 SOCKS

WEAR FOR:

- Keynote speeches
- Master of ceremonies
- Leading training sessions
- Expert appearances

DRESS IT UP
Switch out henley for a white or subtle-print dress shirt.

DRESS IT DOWN
Switch chino for a lighter denim.

EDGE IT UP
Replace loafer with a boot and add some wrist wear or a pendant.

LOOK ㉒ COMPONENTS

TOP LAYERS

 GREY SHAWL COLLAR CARDIGAN

 WHITE HENLEY

PANT

 DARK BURGUNDY CHINO

ACCESSORIES

 NAVY SUEDE DRIVER

 BLACK AND BROWN BELT

 SUNGLASSES

WEAR FOR:

➔ Coffice days

➔ Casual lunches

➔ Working weekends

➔ Client strategy meetings

@AskEmmi TIP | With lighter color pants, black looks very severe in contrast. Go for any other color. Navy makes a nice alternative if you prefer a dark shoe.

DRESS IT UP
Add a cardigan or v-neck sweater.

DRESS IT DOWN
Swap from the leather to a fabric belt.

EDGE IT UP
Switch out for a coated denim and leather shoe.

LOOK ㉓ COMPONENTS

TOP LAYERS

DARK
EMERALD
COTTON-SLUB
T-SHIRT

PANT

LIGHT
DUSTED
LAVENDER
DENIM

ACCESSORIES

NAVY CANVAS STRIPE-
SOLE SLIP-ON

BROWN LEATHER
BELT

WAXED CANVAS BAG

WEAR FOR:

- ➔ Creative casual pitches
- ➔ Gallery openings
- ➔ Any See and Be Seen event

@AskEmmi TIP | A cap-toe boot is an edgier alternative to the cap-toe oxford shoe and looks equally good with denim and slacks.

 DRESS IT UP
Switch from the henley to a dress shirt, add a narrow tie, and untuck pants from boots.

 DRESS IT DOWN
Switch the cap-toe boot to a suede loafer.

EDGE IT UP
Switch out the sweater for a leather jacket.

LOOK ㉔ COMPONENTS

TOP LAYERS

 GREY SUEDE TRIM ZIP-FRONT SWEATER

 WHITE HENLEY

PANT

 TONAL-CAMO PRINT DENIM

ACCESSORIES

 BLACK LEATHER CAP-TOE BOOT

 TWO-TONE BELT

 SOCKS

WEAR FOR:

- Informal lectures
- Executive retreats
- Client lunches
- Out of office meetings

@AskEmmi TIP | A casual tailored vest is a great investment because it goes with chinos, slacks, or denim. It can be worn simply over a button-down or henley, or under a blazer or lightweight jacket.

DRESS IT UP
Add a knit tie and a tie or lapel pin.

DRESS IT DOWN
Remove vest and go with a suede loafer.

EDGE IT UP
Put on some dark grey denim and color shoes.

LOOK ㉕ COMPONENTS

TOP LAYERS

 GREY TAILORED VEST

 GINGHAM BUTTON-DOWN

PANT

 KHAKI DENIM-CUT CHINO

ACCESSORIES

 BROWN BURNISHED-TOE LOAFER

 BROWN LEATHER BELT

 SOCKS

WEAR FOR:

- → Tech events
- → Presentations
- → Conventions
- → Drinks with co-workers

@AskEmmi TIP | You'll get way more compliments and wear out of a well-chosen pair of two-tone shoes than plain lace-ups. Low-contrast combinations with a mixture of textures work best in business settings.

DRESS IT UP
Add grey or black slacks and dark leather shoes.

DRESS IT DOWN
Switch out grey denim for lighter blue.

EDGE IT UP
Add a canvas motorcycle jacket and distressed leather belt.

LOOK 26 COMPONENTS

TOP LAYERS

 DEEP TEAL AND CHALK-STRIPE SWEATER

 NAVY CREW-NECK T-SHIRT

PANT

 DARK GREY DENIM

ACCESSORIES

 TWO-TONE BOOT

 BLUE SUEDE BELT

SOCKS

WEAR FOR:

- → Working meetings
- → Casual lunches
- → Tech meetups
- → Monday-Friday

@AskEmmi TIP | As long as the collars align nicely, you can wear either a crew-neck or a v-neck T-shirt under a v-neck sweater.

DRESS IT UP
Put a pattern button-down underneath the sweater.

DRESS IT DOWN
Switch out loafer for a casual sneaker.

EDGE IT UP
Switch out loafer for a motorcycle boot and a studded belt.

LOOK ❷❼ COMPONENTS

TOP LAYERS

LIGHT GREY GRADIENT V-NECK SWEATER

NAVY V-NECK T-SHIRT

PANT

LIGHT DUSTED LAVENDER DENIM

ACCESSORIES

NAVY SUEDE DRIVER

BROWN LEATHER BELT

SUNGLASSES

WEAR FOR:

→ Casual client dinner

→ Bringing down the house

→ Three cities in two days

@AskEmmi TIP | You can absolutely mix black and brown together. The key is to add other colors into the mix, like grey, burgundy, or dark green.

 DRESS IT UP
Add a pattern button-down and untuck pant from boot.

 DRESS IT DOWN
Switch out sport coat for a sweater.

 EDGE IT UP
Try a dark dress shirt with statement cufflinks. Swap out chinos to a coated denim or print pant.

LOOK ㉘ COMPONENTS

TOP LAYERS

 HEATHER GREY JERSEY BLAZER

 BLACK HENLEY

PANT

 DARK BURGUNDY CHINOS

ACCESSORIES

 BROWN LEATHER WINGTIP BOOT

 BROWN LEATHER BELT

 SOCKS

WEAR FOR:

- ➔ Entrepreneurial meetups
- ➔ Drinks after work
- ➔ Casual meetings
- ➔ Dinner with co-workers

DRESS IT UP
Put on a sweater, vest, or blazer.

DRESS IT DOWN
Switch to light wash denim.

EDGE IT UP
Switch pant to a coated denim and fabric shoe to leather.

LOOK ㉙ COMPONENTS

TOP LAYERS

NAVY AND OLIVE PAISLEY BUTTON-DOWN

PANT

KHAKI DENIM

ACCESSORIES

NAVY CANVAS STRIPE-SOLE SLIP-ON

DISTRESSED LEATHER BELT

SOCKS

WEAR FOR:

- Investor meetings
- Business lunches
- From Manhattan to the Hamptons

DRESS IT UP
Put on slacks instead of denim.

 DRESS IT DOWN
Opt for a lighter color chino.

 EDGE IT UP
Trade the loafers in for navy suede boots.

LOOK ③⓪ COMPONENTS

TOP LAYERS

 LIGHT
BLUE
CHECK
BLAZER

 NAVY
CREW-NECK
T-SHIRT

PANT

 GREY
WASH
DENIM

ACCESSORIES

 LIGHT
BROWN
FAUX CROC
DRIVERS

 STITCHED
BROWN
LEATHER
BELT

 SOCKS

WHAT TO WEAR TO AN INTERVIEW OTHER THAN A SUIT

The predominant advice on the interwebs is that if you have an interview, you wear a suit and tie, even if you're applying for a job at the meatpacking plant. In certain industries like finance and law, it's true that the suit is still king at the interview.

However, it simply isn't the case anymore that a suit is always the best or only choice for interview attire that gets you the job, especially in the tech and startup world. Don't confuse this lack of formality with lack of intention or mission, though. Even at companies where dressing up doesn't matter, your personal image still does.

Show you can understand the nuances and aren't trapped on one of the polar extremes of the spectrum—suit or jeans and a T-shirt—with little clue what's in between. Presentation is everything, even in casual environments, but not in the old way of dressing to the nines to show off. People want authenticity, so dressing in a way that makes you feel comfortable and confident is clutch.

So what is a guy to do in this new grey area of interview dressing? Select the clothes that do these three things:

1. Show that you understand the role.

2. Show how comfortably you fit within the company culture.

3. Make you feel proud to be observed from head to toe so you walk in like the guy they'd be lucky to snag.

Role

Even within the same company there are different expectations for interview attire, so it's about dressing for the role. Take Google for example. According to Christopher Woods, former Head of Global Industry Relations there, the two major hiring sides at Google are sales and engineering. The sales side still expects to see a full suit, but on the engineering side it's a green light for dress denim, button-downs, and sport coats.

Do your research and find out what's appropriate for both day-to-day attire and interview attire. Ask your HR liaison, and if they simply say "business casual," wow them with your level of preparedness by inquiring, "Does that mean dress denim, khakis, or slacks?" They'll usually jump right in with specifics.

But what about at companies that are more casual than that? In those environments, what's acceptable ranges across a much wider spectrum, so in addition to dressing for the role, you have to fit the culture and dress like the most confident version of yourself.

Culture

There's a rise in a new breed of business, the culture-driven company, where the culture is valued equally to the product. No doubt you've heard of these employee meccas with air hockey tables, catered meals and snacks, and re-fresh and recharge lounges, where weary workers are whisked away to their cars in oversized bassinets filled with puppies on the backs of unicorns (that benefit might not be 100% rolled out yet). Walk through the doors of any of those seemingly "anything goes" companies in a suit and you'll suddenly wish you were interviewing at the meatpacking plant.

HubSpot, the world leader in inbound marketing, is just such a progressive company. According to its Head of Creative and Design, Keith Frankel, there is no set expected attire: "We're looking for authenticity and how well you fit with our company culture. You should come in being who you are, but we can tell your intention about working here by how you've put yourself together. You can come in jeans, but we can tell if they're nice jeans or crappy jeans."

"Presentation is still key, but it's not about being pretentious or pompous. Your aesthetic is what we see first, and it sets the tone for how well you'll fit with the company culture. We're not progressive for the sake of being progressive. We believe in companies being more human and authentic in the way they do business, and that culture starts person to person in the office. And what you wear tells us about your personality and how confident you are being yourself."

Thank you, Keith, for that excellent segue into our next section: confidence.

Confidence

Remember the white jacket study? Don't think for a second of wearing something that you don't feel completely awesome and natural in. You can follow the Style 4Mula when dressing for these types of interviews to nail the right look.

Now that you know that what to wear to these non-suit-and-tie interviews depends on the role, the company culture, and how confident it makes you feel, let's take you to four ideas. In terms of flavors of business casual, these are creative casual or tech casual rather than executive or classic, and they are presented in the order of most formal (without a suit) to most relaxed (for the small but still very real segment of the job market that goes in for interviews in jeans and a T-shirt).

Three of these looks are included in the 30 Looks section (bonus points if you can spot the new one), but here we are looking at them through the lens of interviewing and to give you more visual substitutions. Each gets the job done in communicating that you have your s*@! together, and each shows varying degrees of casualness and edge.

The core of most of these looks is the top layer. It's not a bad idea to dress one notch up in case you need it, and this gives you the option to remove that piece in an instant to dress down your look should the scene on the ground be totally casual.

The "I have a few offers but I'm open to seeing how good of a fit your company is for me" ❶

**INTERVIEW
IN THIS FOR:**

→ Senior position
   at a company
   with a relaxed
   and varied attire

@AskEmmi TIP | A casual blazer paired with grey wash denim and a tailored color T-shirt is a tasteful way to communicate you're not the typical business guy. Any skin tone-flattering color T-shirt can be worn under the jacket.

 DRESS IT UP

Try a dress shirt or casual button-down with a dark leather belt and pocket square.

 DRESS IT DOWN

Swap out the bold color for a light grey T-shirt. Do a fabric belt and switch to loafers.

 EDGE IT UP

Go with a dark, subtle-print button-down, tailored vest, and motorcycle boots.

**INTERVIEW
IN THIS FOR:**

- Media agencies
- Tech startups
- Fashion brands

@AskEmmi TIP | Young guys can have a tough time looking more mature without squashing their individuality and their up-and-comer feel. A narrow tie, denim, and a tailored vest strike a great balance. The tucked pant is optional.

 DRESS IT UP

Opt for wool slacks, add a pocket square and cufflinks, and untuck the denim.

 DRESS IT DOWN

Swap out coated denim to light blue jeans, and toss on loafers or drivers and a light brown belt. You can also roll the sleeves, open the top button, and loosen the tie an inch.

 EDGE IT UP

Remove the tie and add a print scarf, or roll the sleeves and don some wrist wear and a fashion sneaker.

**INTERVIEW
IN THIS FOR:**

- Biotech Company
- Engineering firm
- Media agency
- Tech startup

DRESS IT UP

Add a button-down underneath the sweater, a tie, and a dress belt.

 DRESS IT DOWN

Switch from dark jeans to a lighter color denim, opt for a white henley underneath the sweater, and switch the boots to a woven leather espadrille or loafer.

 EDGE IT UP

Toss on a dark button-down underneath the sweater and add a leather jacket and pair of coated denim.

**INTERVIEW
IN THIS FOR:**

→ Anywhere you
can get away with
it you lucky dog

DRESS IT UP

Toss on a sport coat or a button-down and add a neatly-folded pocket square.

DRESS IT DOWN

Put on denim and casual sneakers and a fabric-strap watch.

EDGE IT UP

Add a dark color T-shirt, a bold color suede belt, and a wingtip boot.

THIS ISN'T GOODBYE!

As I sit here at 3 AM on my birthday writing the last bit of this labor of love with my dogs in a deadweight sleep turf war on my lap, I truly hope that you've enjoyed this guide and that it serves you well. Although the pages here will soon be ending, your style metamorphosis is just beginning, and I'm just a click away. You can find me online at www.emmisorokin.com or on Facebook, where you can share your comments about the book. You can also tweet me @AskEmmi, and be sure to tweet out your favorite looks with #BCSG. Lastly, email me through my website and I'll send you three ideas on how to spice up the outfits you want to wear with most men's favorite business casual sidekick, the blue shirt.

GLOSSARY

Accessories: Anything that you wear or carry that does not fall into the pants and tops or jackets and coats categories, like shoes, socks, belt, bag, umbrella, eyewear, etc.

Break: What I need after writing this book. Also, the term for the folds or bends that appear in the lower leg of your pants when you wear them. Your pants will have more or less break depending on how much longer the pant leg is than your actual leg.

Burnished: A type of polished finish. A burnished-toe shoe typically has a darker polish than the base leather color that is applied and then mostly rubbed away. This creates a subtle effect that can be a nice alternative to a plain leather.

Button-down: Can mean two things. I know, I'm sorry, but in this crazy world sometimes words take on multiple meanings, and we can't let bedlam take over. 1. A dress shirt with buttons on the collar. 2. A shirt in a more casual fabric typically in a print that also buttons up at the front (and may also have buttons on the collar) that is cut shorter so it can be worn untucked. Catalogs from the '80s called these sport shirts, which, since their intention was not for sports, clarified nothing—thanks again, '80s. I, like a sane human being, refer to these as casual button-downs.

Casual button-down: See 2. in Button-down.

Casual sneaker: A sneaker designed to be worn outside of the gym. They come in fabric or leather and in all colors. When leaving classic "Chuck Taylors territory" they can start being referred to as fashion sneakers.

Chino: Casual non-denim pants that can come in any color and are made with a cotton twill fabric. If they are a khaki color, you could also call them khakis.

Coated denim: Jeans that have a waxy finish, which makes the denim have a slight to moderate glisten. Sometimes also called waxed denim.

Contrast: When two intentionally different colors are used together. This contrast-collar polo is an example.

Cut: Refers to the fit that a garment will have. Pants, shirts, and blazers come in a variety of cuts, from slim to roomy.

Denim: A pair of jeans. "Wash" refers to the color.

Dress denim: A darker wash denim in a straight cut that is designed to be worn with dressier items like blazers.

Dress shirt: The most formal of button-down shirts. More appropriate for slacks where a casual button-down is better with jeans and chinos.

Driver: A type of loafer with a sole and heel optimized for driving. A driver makes a fantastic casual shoe even when you are on foot, but is not the wisest choice when doing a lot of walking.

Espadrilles: Shoes that are typically slip-ons with a flexible rubber sole and rope detailing around the bottom.

Fashion sneaker: A sneaker designed to be worn outside of the gym. They can be referred to as casual sneakers, but fashion sneakers typically have more design elements.

Feel: In this book, the "feel" of a garment is the tone it sets. Feel affects how appropriate a garment is for its context.

Finish: Refers to any surface treatment done to the fabric or leather or metal. Example: This leather loafer's finish has a bit of shine to it.

Henley: A cotton crew-neck shirt that has a button closure at the top.

Khaki: A tan or beige color. The term "khakis" typically refers to casual non-denim pants (chinos) in that color.

Knit: Refers to the fabric most commonly associated with garments that have give or stretch to them, like sweaters, polos, and hoodies.

Layering: Putting on multiple garments. T-shirt plus a hoodie = two layers. Button-down, vest, and blazer = three layers.

Loafer: A general term for any slip-on shoe that does not require lacing to stay on. Can conjure images of old school tasseled loafers, but shouldn't.

Oxford: A lace-up shoe. They can be dressy or casual. Wingtips are types of oxfords.

Patent Leather: A very glossy finish of leather.

Polo: A short-sleeve cotton shirt with a collar. Ralph Lauren has gotten men confused enough to think that if you wear one of these shirts it should have his logo on it.

Silhouette: The outline of a shape. As a man you always want the most prominent part of your silhouette to be the shoulders.

Sport coat: A casual blazer. This one is made from jersey fabric (what sweatshirts are made from) which adds to its casual factor.

Top layer: The garment you put on last. It can be a sweater, a hoodie, a sport coat, etc.

Two-tone: When a garment or accessory has two colors.

Wrist wear: Any men's bracelet. But men are afraid of bracelets, so now they are called wrist wear.

GUSHY THANK YOU PAGE

To My Family - Without your love, courage, and particular strain of dysfunction, I would not be where I am today. Mom, thank you for everything you sacrificed for us. Natasha, I can't wait to see your exceptional talents come to fruition. Dad, thank you for the life lessons. Ya vas lyublyu.

Ross C.C.C. Miller - Thank you for first seeing and nurturing the entrepreneur in me. You changed the course of my life. What color Murciélago? L&D.

Jamie Ciocco - You are the liquid gold of my life. Without you this book would still be a collection of stick figures on cocktail napkins. Go team!

Andrew Hanson - Thank you for having really great hair and being so passionate about punctuation.

Adam Katz - Thank you for all of your incredibly hard work bringing this book to life, for the copious red wine, and the pillow fights.

Karl Ginter - For your quarterly visits, deft business counsel, and friendship over the years I am deeply grateful.

Adam LoDolce - If you hadn't been wearing skinny jeans that day this book would still be on my to-do list. Thank you for the ignition and push through the early stages.

Matt Simko - My dearest, thank you for your help during the shoot and playing the name game with me. I'm pretty sure you're going to be the next Ellen, but with a beard.

Maggie Antalek - Thank you for being so incredibly talented and fun to work with. No red solo cups on the next shoot, I promise.

Bill Rugg - Zoolander has nothing on you! Thank you for donating your body to fashion. My love to Miss Barley.

Jeff Lahens - Thank you for being a force of good in the fight for men's style, and for simply being a great guy.

Anthony Santio - You deserve all of the champagne and cupcakes in the world.

KC - Pepper bacon.

To my dogs - You don't read that I know of, but in case science maps dog brains in five years and discovers you can, I didn't want you to feel left out. Thank you for being furry, stupendously adorable, and paralyzingly snuggly.

ACKNOWLEDGEMENTS

Written & Styled by Emmi Sorokin

Edited by:
Andrew Hanson
Jamie Ciocco

Photography Credits
Model - Maggie Antalek
Product - Taylor McLelland & Natalie Nicholas
Author - Edson Dias Photography

Book Design Extraordinaire
Adam Katz - www.atomikdesignstudio.com

Illustrations
Jamie Ciocco - www.trendy.com
Natasha Sorokin

DESIGNER CREDITS

Trademarks, product logos, and company names are the property of their respective owners and do not imply specific product and/or vendor endorsement.

AG Adriano Goldschmied
Belstaff
Burberry Britt
Canali
Converse
Diesel
Etro
Hudson
Johnston & Murphy
Paul Smith
Prada
Psycho Bunny
Saks Fifth Avenue Black
Ted Baker
Theory
Tod's
Tom Ford
Vince.
Z Zenga
7 for All Mankind

LITERARY CREDITS

Gladwell, Malcolm (2005). *Blink: The Power of Thinking Without Thinking.* New York, NY: Little, Brown and Company.

Adam, Hajo and Galinsky, Adam (2012). "Enclothed cognition," *Journal of Experimental Social Psychology*, 48, 918-925.

Hutheesing, Nikhil (2012). "The Real Cost of Hiring a Coach," Bloomberg, September 26, slide 7. http://www.bloomberg.com/consumer-spending/2012-09-26/the-real-cost-of-hiring-a-coach.html#slide7.

Made in the USA
Lexington, KY
02 April 2015